IRAN'S NUCLEAR CORE

UNINSPECTED MILITARY SITES

VITAL TO THE NUCLEAR WEAPONS PROGRAM

October 2017

A PUBLICATION OF THE NATIONAL COUNCIL OF RESISTANCE OF IRAN
U.S. REPRESENTATIVE OFFICE

Iran's Nuclear Core: Uninspected Military Sites, Vital to the Nuclear Weapons Program

Copyright © National Council of Resistance of Iran – U.S. Representative Office, 2017.

All rights reserved. No part of this monograph may be used or reproduced in any manner whatsoever without written permission except in the case of brief quotations embodied in articles or reviews.

First published in 2017 by National Council of Resistance of Iran - U.S. Representative Office (NCRI-US), 1747 Pennsylvania Ave., NW, Suite 1125, Washington, DC 20006

ISBN-10: 1-944942-08-4
ISBN-13: 978-1-944942-08-3

ISBN-10 (eBook): 1-944942-09-2L
ISBN-13 (eBook): 978-1-944942-09-0

Library of Congress Control Number: 2017956901

Library of Congress Cataloging-in-Publication Data

National Council of Resistance of Iran - U.S. Representative Office.

Iran's Nuclear Core: Uninspected Military Sites, Vital to the Nuclear Weapons Program

    1. Iran. 2. Nuclear. 3. Revolutionary Guards. 4. Middle East. 5. IAEA

First Edition: October 2017

Printed in the United States of America

TABLE OF CONTENTS

INTRODUCTION

Reliable, comprehensive and robust verification lie at the crux of any arms control agreement. This is particularly true in the case of the Joint Comprehensive Plan of Action (JCPOA), better known to the public as the Iran Nuclear Deal. The deal is between the five permanent members of the United Nations' Security Council, Germany, and the Iranian regime. The agreement rests on verifying aspects of the Iranian regime's nuclear program. However, because of Tehran's aspirations for a nuclear weapon, the bulk of the regime's program has been of a covert military nature. As a result, formulating an arms control agreement to prohibit the regime's access to nuclear arms, as per Iran's Treaty on the Non-Proliferation of Nuclear Weapons (NPT) obligations, has proven a major challenge to the international community.

Access to Military Facilities

One of the key issues of the verification process has been access to Iran's military sites because of the lack of cooperation between the Iranian regime and the international community. The United States Ambassador to the United Nations, Nikki Haley, raised the problem on September 5, 2017, "for decades, the Iranian military conducted a covert nuclear weapons program, undeclared and hidden from international inspectors. In 2002, Iranian dissidents revealed the existence of a uranium enrichment plant and heavy water reactor – both violations of Iran's safeguards agreement with the IAEA [International Atomic Energy Agency]."[1] Referring to the Fordow site, she pointed out that this secret enrichment plant had been hidden by the Iranian regime "deep inside a mountain, deep inside an IRGC [Islamic Revolutionary Guards Corps] base."[2] However, her "biggest concern is that Iranian leaders – the same ones who in the past were caught operating a covert nuclear program at military sites – have stated publicly that they will refuse to allow IAEA inspections of their military sites."[3]

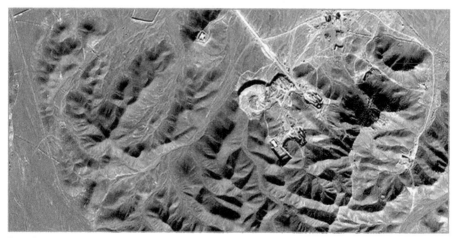

The Fordow enrichment facility was built under a mountain in a military area until it was exposed.

1   Nikki Haley address on Iran and the JCPOA - American Enterprise Institute - September 5, 2017
    http://www.aei.org/publication/nikki-haley-address-on-iran-and-the-jcpoa/

2   Ibid,.

3   Ibid,.

" The biggest concern is that Iranian
leaders — the same ones who in the
past were caught operating a covert nuclear
program at military sites — have stated
publicly that they will refuse to allow
IAEA inspections of their military sites. "

—**Nikki Haley,** *United States Ambassador to the United Nations*

Given the regime's track record as expressed by Haley and others, unfettered access to military facilities is essential to a viable verification process.

The head of the IAEA, Yukiya Amano, told the Associated Press on August 31, 2017, that the agency should have access to military sites. He stressed that under monitoring conditions accepted by Iran, his agency "has access to [all] locations without making distinctions between military and civilian locations," as it works to ensure that Iran doesn't have hidden nuclear activities.[4]

The Iranian regime's highest officials, however, have consistently and categorically rejected any access to military facilities. Ali-Akbar Velayati, a foreign policy advisor to Ali Khamenei, the regime's Supreme Leader, said on September 13, 2017 that "neither Mr. Amano, nor his agents, nor any other foreigner has any right to inspect our military centers, because these centers are prohibited territory... Previous agreements with the Agency were under no circumstances about access to military sites; if they had been, we would not have agreed. Mr. Amano has imagined his claim of such a right."[5]

Velayati said previously, on August 29, "the Americans can take their wish to inspect our military centers under the pretext of JCPOA or any other excuse to their grave."[6]

4 George Jahn, "UN Nuclear Agency Rejects Iran's Stance on Military Sites," U.S. News & World Report, August 31, 2017, https://www.usnews.com/news/world/articles/2017-08-31/un-agency-notes-no-iranian-violations-of-nuclear-deal.

5 "Provincial Reporters: Claiming the Right to Visit Amano's Inventions for Military Centers." Magiran, June 22, 1996, http://www.magiran.com/npview.asp?ID=3627307.

6 Nameh News, 29 August 2017, https://goo.gl/1rcrCe

Damn you, thinking you will ever inspect any of our military centers. We will ram bullets down the throats of anyone who tries to set eyes on the IRGC's centers.

—**Gholamhossein Gheibpour,** *IRGC Brigadier General*

IRGC Major General Hassan Firouzabadi, top military advisor to the Supreme Leader, said on August 27, 2017 that "in the Islamic Republic of Iran, no official, foreign or Iranian, nor even other unrelated members of the armed forces, can inspect our military centers except with the permission of the Commander in Chief."[7]

IRGC Brigadier General Gholamhossein Gheibparvar, the commander of *Bassij*, affiliated with the IRGC, said on September 3, 2017, "raising this issue is simply a joke and is rejected outright, since military centers are considered as the honor of the armed forces."[8]

On May 30, 2015, when he was the commander of IRGC in Fars Province (south Iran), he said "damn you, thinking you will ever inspect any of our military centers. We will ram bullets down the throats of anyone who tries to set eyes on the IRGC's centers."[9]

This all begs a simple question. **Why does the Iranian regime so vociferously oppose this key verification article?**

7 Fars News Agency, September 23, 2017, http://www.farsnews.com/newstext. php?nn=13960605001593

8 Entekhab News, September 3, 2017, https://goo.gl/CkiWto

9 Fars News Agency, May 30, 2015, http://www.farsnews.com/printable. php?nn=13940309001543

Findings of Iranian Resistance

The Iranian Resistance, relying on the network of the People's Moja-hedin Organization of Iran (PMOI/MEK) inside Iran, in particular its vast network of sources in the Iranian regime's various civilian and military enti-ties, has been scrutinizing the regime's nuclear program from various aspects since 1991.[10]

Over a quarter of a century, PMOI/MEK has made more than one hundred revelations of secret sites, projects, procurements, and key figures involved in the regime's nuclear program. PMOI/MEK information on var-ious aspects of the nuclear project, including enrichment, weaponization, and missile delivery systems, indicates that Tehran has worked systematically on the various stages of enrichment, weaponization, warheads, and delivery systems. In other words, Iran has been preparing itself to obtain a nuclear weapon.

Deception, concealment, lying, destroying and tampering with evidence, stage-managing, fabricating stories and creating narratives have all been consistent features of the Iranian regime's handling of its nuclear program, whether with regard to the Iranian people or the international community.

The Iranian regime has been working at five sites to enrich uranium at various quantities and method. These sites include Natanz, Arak, Lash-kar-Abad, Shian-Lavisan, and the previously mentioned Fordow.[11] Tehran

---

10 Robert Novak, Rowland Evans, "Beijing's Tehran Connection," The Washington Post, June 26, 1991, http://www.washingtonpost.com/archive/opinions/1991/06/26/beijings-teh-ran-connection/371737c9-fbcc-4906-82c5-b687cc0aca72/

11 Lashkarabad in Karaj (west of Tehran) was the site of a laser program that was used for re-search and advancement of laser isotopes. Tehran had concealed its existence. It was exposed by the National Council of Resistance of Iran in May 2003. Before the IAEA visit three months later, the regime moved the laser enrichment equipment to the nuclear research center in Karaj used for agricultural and medical purposes. In November 2003, however, the IAEA said, "Iran acknowledged that the uranium metal had been intended not only for the production of shield-ing material, as previously stated, but also for use in the laser enrichment programme."

Lavisan-shian, located in north Tehran housed the first headquarters in charge of weap-onization of the nuclear program, called Physics Research Center (PHRC). The National Council of Resistance of Iran revealed the existence of Shian in May 2003. Tehran subse-quently moved the headquarters from that venue and razed the place, before the IAEA was granted access to the site in June 2004.

has not provided the IAEA with information on any of these sites or projects, much less declaring them in the early stages or on its own initiative. The Iranian regime only acknowledges the existence of such sites after their existence and activities are brought to the international community's attention by revelations of the Iranian Resistance or other sources.[12]

12 Alireza Jafarzadeh, "Is verification regime enforceable on Iran's nuclear program?" The Hill, April 23, 2015, http://thehill.com/blogs/congress-blog/foreign-policy/239763-is-verification-regime-enforceable-on-irans-nuclear.

TWO NUCLEAR PROGRAMS OF IRAN

In the course of the past twenty-five or so years, the Iranian Resistance has determined that two systems have been fully functional. One is an overt program, civilian in nature that includes the Atomic Energy Organization of Iran (AEOI), universities and academic institutions. The second is a military program that is clandestine and concealed. Consequent to extensive research and review by the Iranian Resistance, the relationship between the two programs has become clear.

Contrary to the original, classic perception, the two systems do not function as parallel systems. Rather, they resemble two concentric circles, working in tandem. The military aspect of the program has been and remains at the heart of Iran's nuclear activities.

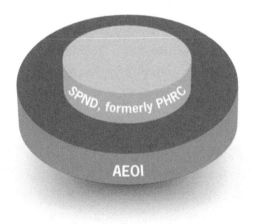

Features of the Iranian regime's nuclear program: The relationship between the civilian and military sectors

The civilian sector of the program has systematically provided a plausible logistical cover for the military sector, and acts as a conduit for it. The results of the research, accomplishments, and advancements of the civilian program have been directed to the military, which has ultimately benefitted from all such achievements.

The military sector has gone through changes in name, location, and reorganizations over the years. However, it has never halted its work, and key figures in the sector have remained unchanged.

To control information and prevent leaks, in addition to making use of past experience, specific companies affiliated with or belonging to the IRGC or the Defense Ministry have carried out the construction of the sites involved in the nuclear project.[13]

An important feature of the Iranian regime's nuclear program is that several sites and centers where nuclear related activities are conducted are situated in sprawling military complexes that also house scores of tunnels and silos. This not only makes IAEA access to these locations more difficult, but makes it possible to relocate these centers and projects to other locations within the vast military complex. As such, if it becomes necessary to relocate a project or center, it can easily be moved to a different silo or tunnel within the parameters of the military site. This makes pinpointing the exact location of nuclear research and activities more challenging, and reduces the chance of exposure.

The civilian sector has provided a plausible cover, by establishing nuclear energy projects at the universities. Resources and research can be used on the one hand, and their experts and talented individuals trained and recruited on the other. It has also provided a conduit for procuring dual-purpose technology and equipment that is ultimately used in the military section.

---

13 Sites such as "Pazhouheshkadeh" (Research Academy at Plan 6 of Parchin) and Haft-e-Tir are among sites that have been constructed by specific companies of the Defense Ministry or by companies that are affiliated to the Khatam al-Anbiya, which belongs to the IRGC.

Scores of authorities and senior officials of the two systems have exchanged positions and responsibilities over the years. It has been common practice to utilize scientists and researchers in the civilian side for the military program, and to lend staff from the military side to the civilian sector to increase proficiency and expertise by utilizing each other's facilities and centers. As such, universities affiliated with Iran's Islamic Revolutionary Guard Corps (IRGC) and the Ministry of Defense, Imam Hossein University and Malek-Ashtar University, have played an important role as a bridge between these two programs.[14]

A review of the military sector's methods in obtaining essential equipment and devices revealed that on several occasions even the postal addresses of universities and academic centers affiliated with the civilian nuclear project have been used for procurement purposes. Some entities at the highest levels of the Iranian regime, including offices and centers affiliated with the President's office, have been involved in smuggling or skirting sanctions to obtain illicit or dual-purpose equipment for these projects.

For instance, the IAEA report on February 22, 2008, pointed out "Iran stated that the AEOI had encountered difficulties with procurement because of international sanctions imposed on the country, and that that was why the AEOI had requested the Dean of the university to assist in the procurement of a UF6 mass spectrometer. According to Iran, in 1988, the Dean of the university approached the Head of the Mechanics Workshop of the Shahid Hemmat Industrial Group (SHIG), which belonged to the Ministry of Sepah, and asked him to handle the procurement. According to Iran, the mass spectrometer was never delivered."[15] The Head of the Mechanics Workshop was Seyed Abbas Shahmoradi- Zavareh, who was later appointed as the Head of Physics Research Center, the first headquarters of the weaponization aspect of the nuclear project, when it was established in 1989. In fact, various equipment and devices that were imported and purchased ostensibly for universities remain unaccounted for.

14 Imam Hossein University of the IRGC, www.ihu.ac.ir; Malek-Ashtar University of Technology, affiliated to the Defense Ministry, www.mut.ac.ir.=

15 Implementation of the NPT Safeguards Agreement and relevant provisions of Security Council resolutions 1737 (2006) and 1747 (2007) in the Islamic Republic of Iran, report by the Director General of the IAEA, February 22, 2008, https://www.iaea.org/sites/default/files/gov2008-4.pdf

Background of key figures

The research on nuclear weapons was initiated from the IRGC research center in the 1980s. Several of the IRGC's most senior officers and top brass have been following this project from its inception closely over the years.[16]

The backgrounds of some key figures in the Iranian regime's nuclear program are telling of the true nature of the nuclear program. During the formation and advancement of the nuclear program, these characters functioned interchangeably within the military and/or the civilian sectors, depending on specific needs of the program.

- **Dr. Fereydoun Abbasi Davani** is one of these individuals. He enrolled in the IRGC at its inception[17]. He received his MS in nuclear physics in 1987 and his PhD in 2002, and is an expert in laser technology. As such, he has been involved in the project of enriching uranium, using lasers. Abbasi has been one of the key figures in the military section, where he has played an active role from the inception of the

---

16 James Dunn "'It's like letting a murderer investigate his own murder': The man who used to be in charge of Iran's nuclear weapons is tipped for a new job... certifying to the UN that they don't exist," *DailyMail*, August 22, 2015, http://www.dailymail.co.uk/news/article-3207152/It-s-like-letting-murderer-investigate-murder-man-charge-nuclear-weapons-Iran-trusted-inspections-according-secret-deal.html.

Testimonies and eye-witness accounts by scores of individuals who have been directly involved in the nuclear project point to the reality that the top brass of the IRGC have been involved in the nuclear project of the clerical regime from the inception of the project and have been overseeing it. https://ncr-iran.org/en/news/nuclear/248-iran-has-completed-the-techniques-and-know-how-necessary-for-assembling-a-nuclear-bomb

The National Council of Resistance in a press conference in Paris on November 17, 2004 revealed that IRGC Brigadier General Ali Hosseini-Tash, then the Deputy Defense Minister, oversaw the nuclear weapons project. https://www.ncr-iran.org/en/news/nuclear/18980-ncri-revelation-iran-regime-s-top-nuclear-weapons-official-counterpart-of-iaea-for-inspection-of-parchin

During Ahmadinejad's tenure, Hosseini-Tash became the deputy secretary of the Supreme National Security Council for Strategic Affairs. The Supreme National Security Council is the most senior decision-making body on national security matters. It was very telling that Hosseini-Tash signed the agreement between the regime and the IAEA for the UN watchdog to inspect the section of the Parchin site suspected of being used for high explosive tests related to a nuclear trigger mechanism.

17 Biography of Fereydoun Abbasi Davani, Massolin website, https://goo.gl/h2GuJo

Fereydoun Abbasi during the Iran-Iraq war.

Fereydoun Abbasi, former Head of the Atomic Energy Organization of Iran.

weaponization headquarters. He has been active in recruiting suitable individuals for the military nuclear project since the early 1990s.[18]

By his own acknowledgment, his real rank in the IRGC is "general."[19] He became a member of the faculty of the Physics Department of Imam Hossein University in 1993 and was named Dean of the Physics Department. But according to the state-run media, he rarely showed up at the university and evidently spent most of his time in another venue, i.e. the headquarters for the weaponization of the nuclear project. He became the head of the civilian sector, the AEOI on February 13, 2000, a post he held until August 2013.

- **Mohsen Fakhrizadeh Mahabadi** (known as **Dr. Mohseni** within the regime), the current head of the Organization of Defensive Innovation and Research (*Sazman-e Pazhouheshhaye Novin-e Defa'i*), known by its Persian acronym SPND, the entity in charge of weaponization, has a similar background. He is an IRGC Brigadier General and has played various roles in the nuclear

Mohsen Fakhrizadeh

18 Mashreg News, Interview with Fereydoun Abbasi, December 22, 2010, https://goo.gl/JWSMPn

19 ISNA News Agency, August 19, 2013, goo.gl/2Kx6Ue

weapons program. The National Council of Resistance of Iran exposed his identity in a press conference in Paris on November 17, 2004.[20] The IAEA has for years requested to interview Fakhrizadeh for his unique role in the nuclear weapons program, but the regime has vehemently rejected this request.[21]

20 "Modern Defensive Readiness and Technology Center," *GlobalSecurity.org*, July 24, 2011, https://www.globalsecurity.org/wmd/world/iran/tehran-mdrtc.htm.

21 Fredrik Dahl, "U.N. nuclear report puts Iran 'mystery man' in spotlight," *Reuters*, November 11, 2011, http://www.reuters.com/article/us-nuclear-iran-fakhrizadeh/u-n-nuclear-report-puts-iran-mystery-man-in-spotlight-idUSTRE7AA43J20111111.

Organizational Chart of The Organization of Defensive Innovation and Research in Charge of Manufacturing Nuclear Bomb

Sazman-e Pazhouheshhaye Novin-e Defa'i (SPND)

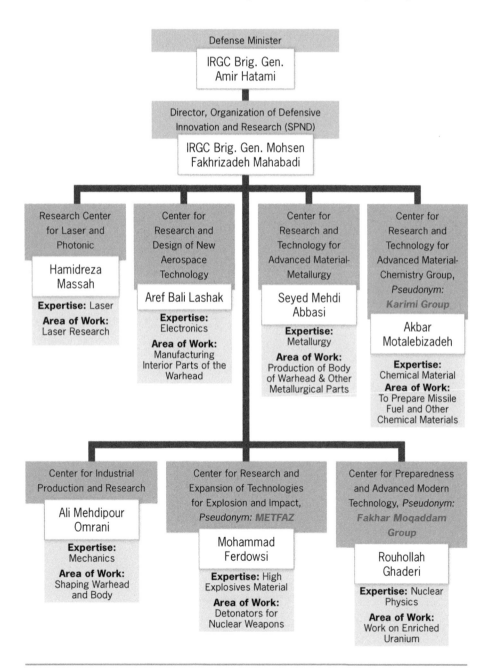

MILITARY SITES SUSPECTED OF INVOLVEMENT IN THE NUCLEAR PROGRAM

The Iranian Resistance, has identified the following sites in recent years that, with high degrees of certainty, have been involved in various aspects of the nuclear weapons project:

1. **Pazhouheshkadeh** (affiliated with METFAZ)- located at the Parchin military complex (southeast Tehran)

2. **Nouri Industrial site** – located at Khojir military complex (southeast Tehran)

3. **Hafte Tir site** – located in the Hafte Tir military complex

4. **Sanjarian site** (affiliated with METFAZ)- in the vicinity of the Parchin military complex

These sites and their nuclear projects are either controlled by or working in close cooperation with SPND, the headquarters of which is in two centers near the Defense Ministry in Tehran at the Nour (light) complex and the Mojdeh site.

Pazhouheshkadeh (affiliated with METFAZ)

SPND is comprised of 7 subdivisions, each of which carries out a certain portion of nuclear weapons research. The unit responsible for conducting research and building a trigger for a nuclear weapon is called the Center for Research and Expansion of Technologies for Explosion and Impact (*Markaz-e Tahghighat va Tose'e Fanavari-e Enfejar va Zarbeh*), known by its Farsi acronym METFAZ.[22] The director of this unit is currently an engineer named Mohammad Ferdowsi, who has been working at the Defense Ministry since 1986 and is a high-explosives expert. At the same time, he is the chairman of the board of directors of the High-Explosives Society of Malek Ashtar University.

The most recent investigation by the Iranian Resistance revealed that METFAZ has transferred its main activities to another location, which had remained secret until April 21, 2017, when the National Council of Resistance of Iran exposed it.[23] New intelligence revealed the existence of a new location, which is identified in SPND's internal communications with the codename "Research Academy" (*Pazhouheshkadeh*), as well as the codename "Research" (*Tahghighat*). This location has become the main center for METFAZ's tests and other activities.

Following the nuclear agreement (JCPOA) in 2015, the regime sought to avoid blowing the cover on METFAZ's activities. Consequently, a large portion of the activities conducted at METFAZ in Sanjarian, as well as the personnel working at the site, were transferred to the Research Academy situated within Parchin. The move resulted in a lessening of activities at the Sanjarian site. The Iranian regime has done its utmost to keep the Research Academy, which is an important site, a secret from international organizations.

The move was based on the conclusion reached by regime officials that the probability of the IAEA's gaining future access to Parchin is very low,

22 Edward Cody, "Exiles Accuse Iran of Working on Nuclear Detonators at 2 Sites," *The Washington Post*, September 25, 2009, http://www.washingtonpost.com/wp-dyn/content/article/2009/09/24/AR2009092404815.html.

23 Press conference by the US Representative Office of the National Council of Resistance of Iran, April 21, 2017, http://ncrius.org/revelations-status-iran-regimes-nuclear-bomb-making-apparatus.html

Parchin Military Complex at South East Tehran

Plan 6 Zeinoddin in Parchin military complex

Imagery of Plan 6 area in Parchin

which means that the site is an optimal location for activities the regime seeks to shield from view.

Parchin, where the Research Academy is located, is a large military district controlled by the Defense Ministry about 30 miles south east of Tehran. It contains 12 military and missile complexes. The Defense Ministry calls each one of these industrial units a "Plan" (*Tarh*); specifically, they are code-named Plan 1, through Plan 12.

In light of the sprawling size and existence of various projects and industries, Parchin has been an ideal venue for such an activity over the years, especially since it is practical to conceal a specific project in one particular area and subsequently transfer it to a new location within the complex.

The METFAZ center is situated at Plan 6 of the Parchin military industries complex. The geographical area of the unit (plan) is about 500 acres. It is completely fenced in and fully protected. To conceal the true nature of its work, the Research Academy conducts its research and activities under the cover of conventional research and tests related to Plan 6. Known as Zeinoddin Industries, Plan 6 is a part of the chemical industries of Parchin complex.

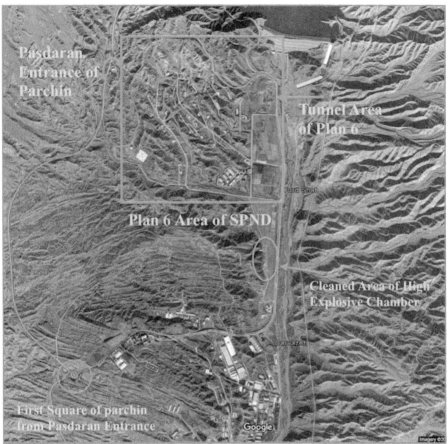

Plan 6 of Parchin as well as other sections in the vicinity

In early 2005, work to build tunnels to accommodate the activities of METFAZ began at Plan 6. Pars Garma, an established company within the regime's military industries, built the tunnels.[24]

One of the managers directly involved in the building of SPND tunnels in Plan 6 district of Parchin was an engineer named Abbas Rashidpour. An employee of Pars Garma, Rashidpour was the manager of the METFAZ Plan 6 project. The construction project took four years to complete. The facilities were handed over to the main client, SPND, METFAZ section, in 2009.

---

24 The CEO of the company is currently Mojtaba Qanbari. The address of this company in Tehran is: Sadr Highway, Manzarieh exit, Erfani Ave, number 46.

Since 2015, the bulk of METFAZ's activities, including those at Sanjarian site, have been transferred to Plan 6 in Zeinoddin industries at Parchin, where they have various silos and factories. The Research Academy is located at the heart of Plan 6. Employees and personnel at the site enter and exit the facilities through the "Gate of Plan 6." However, the Research Academy itself is completely independent and closed off.

One of the main controversies surrounding Parchin is the issue of high explosive vessels and tests with high explosives for a potential nuclear trigger. From early 2012, the IAEA began making requests to visit that specific section of Parchin. Eventually, after extensive modifications and sanitation of the location by the regime, the IAEA was able to have very limited access with all sorts of restrictions at the end of 2015.

It is worth noting that the chamber related to high explosives relevant to the regime's nuclear projects and specifically the high-explosive trigger, was overseen by METFAZ, which ran the activities related to tests with the help of Ukrainian experts.[25] The location of the high explosive chamber and preliminary tests for explosions, which was razed during 2013 and 2014, is at the southern part of the Research Academy at around 700 meters from it.

In order to avoid intelligence leaks about the Research Academy of Zeinoddin, the location is under heavy surveillance and control by the IRGC Intelligence's protection service. The commander of the intelligence protection of this section is Brig. Gen. Mostafa Siri, who is also SPND's head of counter-intelligence.

Brig. Gen. Mostafa Siri

Siri has been Defense Ministry counterintelligence official since 1999. Since the protection of intelligence relative to SPND is extremely sensitive for the Defense Ministry, for the past several years, Siri has been appointed as the head of the counterintelligence unit of SPND. He has recruited a number of trusted allies, including several of his relatives, to work in METFAZ and SPND counter-intelligence units.

25 "Agency claims Iran still working toward nukes," *Fox News,* November 8, 2014, http://www. foxnews.com/world/2014/11/08/agency-claims-iran-still-working-toward-nukes.html.

Nouri Industry and Hemmat Missile Industrial Group

The project to actively pursue production of nuclear warheads is conducted in Khojir by the Hemmat Missile Industries Group. Khojir is a completely secured and vast region southeast of Tehran, covering an area of 120 square kilometers. (The length is approximately 20 km and the average width is 6 km.)

Construction of secret military sites in this location began in 1989 upon Khamenei's orders. The location primarily works on the manufacturing of ballistic missiles such as Shahab 3.

The project to manufacture nuclear warheads, overseen by SPND, is called Alireza Nouri (Nuri) Industry (also referred to as Shahid Nouri Industry), which is one of the industrial branches of the Hemmat Missile Industrial Group.

Due to the extreme sensitivity of manufacturing nuclear warheads, Nouri Industry has its own security and Military Police; individuals who have clearance to other parts of Khojir site are not allowed to go to this section. The entrances to this section are closed and all coming and going is controlled.

General area of Khojir

Parking entrance for Nouri Industry

Nouri Industries involved in developing nuclear warhead – original location

According to reliable reports, scores of large underground tunnels have been constructed in this military complex. The availability of several underground tunnels provides the possibility and flexibility of covering up the activities of the warhead project, or transferring it to a different location in the complex.

The warheads are being designed for installation on Shahab 3 missiles. The most advanced version of Shahab 3 has a range of 2,000 kilometers.

Shahab 3 missile capable of carrying a nuclear warhead

Dr. Mehdi Naghian Fesharaki is a key figure in this project. An expert with computers and electronics, he oversees designs for the construction of a nuclear warhead. Dozens of other experts, including experts in the fields of aerodynamics, structure, and electronics cooperate with him.

North Korean experts cooperate with the regime's experts in this project and have provided significant assistance in the project's progress. The North Korean experts have been particularly helpful in designing the aerodynamics aspects and the shape of the warhead. The North Korean experts have also provided the design for the Hemmat site, its tunnels, and underground centers.[26]

The Iranian Resistance revealed Nouri Industry in 2008,[27] and in 2010, the IAEA confirmed that Iran has worked on Warheads.[28]

Since then, the Iranian Resistance has received reports indicating the relocation of this project to a different place within Khojir complex.

---

26 Press conference by the US Representative Office of the National Council of Resistance of Iran, Washington, DC, June 20, 2017

   http://ncrius.org/wp-content/uploads/2017/06/NCRIUS-Acceleration-of-Missile-Program-of-Iran-20June2017-2.pdf

27 Marc Champion, "Exile Group Claims Iran Is Developing Nuclear Warheads," *The Wall Street Journal*, February 20, 2008, https://www.wsj.com/articles/SB120347970360479423

28 David E. Sanger, William J. Broad, "Inspectors Say Iran Worked on Warhead," *The New York Times*, February 18, 2010, http://www.nytimes.com/2010/02/19/world/middleeast/19iran.html.

Hafte Tir (7th of Tir) Industries in Isfahan

The Hafte Tir site belongs to the Defense Ministry and is located in the military zone of the Hafte Tir Military Industrial Complex near the city of Isfahan in a mountainous area. It is adjacent to the Isfahan-Shiraz highway, about 10 km (six miles) from the town of Mobarakeh, which is 40 km (25 miles) southwest of Isfahan.

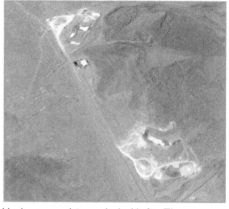

Underground tunnels in Hafte Tir

The site was constructed in complete secrecy under the supervision of SPND and Imam Hossein University of the IRGC. Imam Hossein University has been a key research center for the nuclear weapons projects; the results of its research are provided to SPND, especially to benefit MET-FAZ. SPND and Imam Hossein University experts have visited this site on

Hafte Tir military Complex near Isfahan

Hafte Tir Military Industrial Complex under the supervision of SPND

scores of occasions. IRGC Brigadier General Mohsen Fakhrizadeh, the key official in the regime's nuclear weapons program, directly supervised the construction of this site.

In addition to all of its security advantages and its location far removed from public sight, the fact that it is part of a sprawling military complex provides the possibility of relocating within the complex and covering up the transfer without raising any suspicion. This makes pinpointing the exact location of the activities of the site even more difficult.

To access the site, one has to pass through four layers of security and check-points. The first two checkpoints are at the entrance of the Hafte Tir complex.

In addition to the Defense Ministry's Counter-intelligence Department, the Ministry of Intelligence has a robust presence and directly supervises the site's security safeguards.

The research site related to nuclear activities is located inside of a tunnel, which is about 600 meters (about 0.4 miles) and contains four galleries. This location – with a tunnel for the entrance and one for the exit – is very suitable for its objective. Since Hafte Tir military industries in Isfahan constitutes a major part of the regime's ammunition production, the cover of a conventional military site (normally sealed off from the outside world) protects the work and keeps it secret.

The engineering firm, Ghorb Ghaem, which is one of the IRGC's Khatam al-Anbia (KAA) Headquarters companies, was tasked with constructing this site. The KAA is on the U.S. sanctions list.[29] IRGC Colonel Heydari from the KAA was the construction manager of the site. Colonel Madanizadeh, Deputy Director of the Defense Ministry's Engineering Organization, supervised the project.

The Resistance's probe proved that the same individuals and officials involved in the construction of the Fordow enrichment site were also directly involved in the construction of this site. The Iranian Resistance exposed the then secret uranium enrichment site of Fordow in the vicinity of Qom in 2005,[30] and its existence was confirmed in 2009.[31]

The Fordow site was originally a military site until it was revealed, and eventually the international community exerted enough pressure to gain access to the site.

After the revelation of this site by the Resistance, the Iranian regime made some changes in the location and activities of this project in the Hafte Tir complex.

Workshops at the Hafte Tir were used in the past to produce centrifuge components such as rotor cylinders. In addition to activities in tunnels, the site still has a capability to produce those components clandestinely.

---

29 The Khatam-al-Anbiya Construction Headquarters (KAA) conglomerate is the biggest construction firm in Iran and is owned by the IRGC. It was placed under the US sanctions in October 2007 according to Executive Order 13382.

30 "Iran's Secret Tunnel Project to Conceal Its Nuclear Programs," *Irannuclear.org*, December 20, 2005, http://irannuclear.org/index2.php?option=com_content&do_pdf=1&id=32; The National Council of Resistance of Iran in press conferences in Paris and London on December 20, 2005, exposed the existence of a new secret site in the vicinity of Qom. The revelation was covered by the news agencies. The Associated Press, among others, reported: "Resistance group claims Iran building secret underground nuclear facilities."

31 The existence of a secret site in Fordow was confirmed in a joint press conference of President Obama, Gordon Brown (the Prime Minister of the UK at the time), and Nicholas Sarkozy (the French President at the time) in Pittsburgh on September 25, 2009.

Sanjarian Site

Until recently, this site was the main testing site of METFAZ, one of the sub-divisions of SPND. As explained in the section about *Pazhouheshka-deh*, METFAZ is focused on explosives and trigger mechanisms for nuclear weapons. This entity has a command center and several affiliate centers in and around Tehran.

METFAZ has three main sections, research, production, and test.

One of METFAZ's main locations for research, tests, and experiments is located in the Khojir military district[32], in Khojir military road towards the Parchin military industries, adjacent to Sanjarian village. This site is east of Tehran, on the banks of the Jajrood River, and is known as the Sanjarian site. Sanjarian village is 10 kilometers south of the end of Babaie Highway, adjacent to a military road. There is a metal bridge on the south bank of the river, prior to the passage of the military road from the bridge; a paved road turns to the east. The site is about 500 meters off the military road.

The site is built on the mountain range, at the junction of the river and a tributary of the river. To conceal the activities inside the site, it is surrounded by very high pre-fabricated concrete walls, blocking any view from outside. Tunnels have been built in the site for secret research. The entrance of the site, which is about 170 meters by 170 meters, is on the southeastern side of the building.

A major portion of the tests and experiments that used to be conducted at Sanjarian, have recently been transferred to *Pazhouheshkadeh* in Parchin. While Sanjarian is still functional, it has become semi-active as of late.

---

32 Khojir site is located in eastern Tehran near Jajroud River. There are two missile industry complexes within this site: Hemmat and Bakeri. These are the main locations for the manufacturing of the regime's ballistic missiles. Both of these industrial complexes include several factories and manufacturing units, which are located in tunnels and underground facilities.

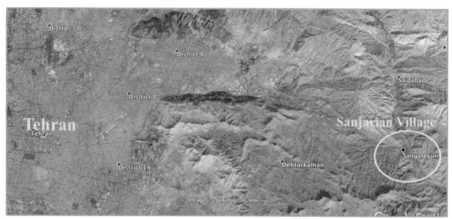

NCRI exposed METFAZ location near Sanjarian Village in 2009.

METFAZ near Sanjarian village

ENTITY RESPONSIBLE FOR COMMAND AND DESIGN OF THE NUCLEAR WEAPONS PROGRAM – SPND

As noted, comprehensive and robust verification is key to guaranteeing the clerical regime's adherence to the nuclear agreement and abandonment of its drive to obtain nuclear weapons. Section T of Annex 1 of the JCPOA (Annex 1- page 27) is of special significance since all the activities that can be related to design and obtaining a nuclear related explosive device are within the purview of this section.[33]

The Section T, titled "Activities which could contribute to the design and development of a nuclear explosive device", underscores:

- 82. Iran will not engage in the following activities which could contribute to the development of a nuclear explosive device:

- 82.1. Designing, developing, acquiring, or using computer models to simulate nuclear explosive devices.

- 82.2. Designing, developing, fabricating, acquiring, or using multi-point explosive detonation systems suitable for a nuclear explosive device, unless approved by the Joint Commission for non-nuclear purposes and subject to monitoring.

- 82.3. Designing, developing, fabricating, acquiring, or using explosive diagnostic systems (streak cameras, framing cameras and flash x-ray cameras) suitable for the development of a nuclear explosive

33 Full text of the Joint Comprehensive Plan of Action, United States Department of State, July 14, 2015, https://www.state.gov/e/eb/tfs/spi/iran/jcpoa/

device, unless approved by the Joint Commission for non-nuclear purposes and subject to monitoring.

- 82.4. Designing, developing, fabricating, acquiring, or using explosively driven neutron sources or specialized materials for explosively driven neutron sources.

Hence, the implementation of the Section T and Tehran's adherence to its content is of critical importance. Within the Iranian regime, the entity directing the quest for nuclear weaponization mentioned in Section T has pursued the technology required for a nuclear weapon for more than two decades. This has been done using different names and different structures. At different junctures, primarily due to revelations blowing its cover, it has relocated and has gone through several reorganizations. But as mentioned earlier, its key personnel have remained intact.

In February 2011, this entity was consolidated under a new organization called the Organization of Defensive Innovation and Research (SPND). In order to expedite the attainment of nuclear weapons, its status and

Mojdeh Site, original headquarters of SPND

organization within the Defense Ministry was elevated. It is currently an independent organization within the Defense Ministry, headed by an IRGC Brigadier General who functions as a Deputy Defense Minister and reports directly to the Defense Minister.

The Iranian Resistance revealed SPND's existence in July 2011.[34] The IAEA provided an extensive review of the possible military dimensions of the Iranian nuclear program as an annex to its November 2011 report. In that report, the IAEA confirmed the existence of SPND.[35] Three years later, on August 29, 2014, the U.S. State Department placed SPND on its sanctions list in accordance with Executive Order 13382.[36]

As mentioned, SPND oversees the issues mentioned in the Section T of the JCPOA. It is comprised of 7 subdivisions, each of which conducts a certain portion of nuclear weapons research. Based on specific reports from each of the subdivisions, all of them are continuing their work on the same scale as prior to the 2015 nuclear agreement.

Mojdeh Site – the original venue of SPND's headquarters

Tehran- Lavizan- Mojdeh Avenue- across Koy-e Nobonyad, known as Mojdeh site, was the original venue of SPND. Some research and some of the workshops of a civilian nature have been kept in this venue.

34 Vahid Salemi, "Opposition: Iran consolidates nuclear bomb effort," *USA Today*, July 23, 2011, https://usatoday30.usatoday.com/news/washington/2011-07-23-iran-nuclear-program_n.htm#mainstory.

35 Implementation of the NPT Safeguards Agreement and relevant provisions of Security Council resolutions in the Islamic Republic of Iran, Report by the Director General, IAEA, November 8, 2011, https://www.iaea.org/sites/default/files/gov2011-65.pdf

36 Additional Sanctions Imposed by the Department of State Targeting Iranian Proliferators, United Stated Department of State, Office of the Spokesperson, August 29, 2014, https://2009-2017.state.gov/r/pa/prs/ps/2014/231159.htm

Nour Building SPND HQ

Nour (Light) Building

SPND headquarters has been moved to Tehran- Pasdaran Ave- Nobon-yad Square- Hossein Langari Avenue (Aghdassieh) Ave- Sanay-e (Lakpour) Avenue - across from Chamran Hospital. In internal communications within the regime, this place is called the Nour Building. The new location has several features:

1. First, it is a secure area under full surveillance.

2. Second, it is located in between several centers and offices affiliated with the Defense Ministry, including the Defense Ministry itself, Al-ghadir Industries (part of the Defense industries; Farsi acronym Sa-sad), the IRGC Union, the sports organization of the Defense Ministry, two residential quarters affiliated with the Defense Ministry, and Chamran Hospital, affiliated with the Defense Ministry.

3. Third, the area is secured by an air defense system.

Nour Bldg and Mojdeh Site of SPND

The distance between the new venue and the old venue is about 1.5 kilometers aerial and about 3 kilometers by road.

CONCLUSION

When the nuclear agreement was reached in 2015, it was described as "the most robust and intrusive inspections and transparency regime ever negotiated for any nuclear program in history."[37]

However, specific intelligence relating to the above four facilities and two headquarters confirms that a significant portion of the various aspects of Iran's nuclear project have been conceived and developed over the past decades in its military centers. It is, therefore, naïve and delusional to speak of verifying Iran's adherence to the JCPOA unless unfettered, prompt access to inspect its military sites is guaranteed and utilized. Otherwise, the world faces a clear and immediate threat to regional and international stability and peace.

The following measures are necessary:

1 Immediate, complete, simultaneous and unfettered inspection of all six sites and centers associated with SPND by the IAEA and the full disclosure of the results as soon as possible. We stress the simultaneity of the inspection of the six sites to preclude any attempt to hide, remove, or sanitize traces relating to illicit nuclear activities. The inspection should include simultaneous and unfettered access to all parts and sections of the large military complexes without limitation.

---

37 President Obama's full remarks announcing a 'framework' for a nuclear deal with Iran, The Washington Post, April 2, 2015, https://www.washingtonpost.com/news/post-politics/wp/2015/04/02/president-obamas-full-remarks-announcing-a-framework-for-a-nuclear-deal-with-iran/?utm_term=.907992f9f391

2 Speedy inspection of any other location, including military sites, suspected of involvement in the Iranian military nuclear project.

3 The IAEA must have access to and interview all scientists and experts involved in Iran's military nuclear project, including Mohsen Fakhrizadeh Mahabadi, Fereiydoun Abbasi Davani, and the heads of SPND's subdivisions. This requirement is fundamental and very obvious. The IAEA cannot definitively clarify the regime's military nuclear program without such interviews.

4 The Agency should reveal any information about SPND's involvement in illicit nuclear activities and its relations with foreign parties, such as its technical cooperation with North Korea. All state parties who have in the past given up their military nuclear programs have made full disclosures of those programs to the Agency. Any hesitation or intransigence by Tehran to reveal its program should be viewed as proof that the mullahs do not intend to put aside their aspirations for a nuclear weapon, and are only playing for time to catch the international community off-guard and achieve their ultimate goal.

APPENDIX A

Notable Nuclear Revelations of the Iranian Resistance

(1991-2017)

Since 1991 the Iranian resistance has exposed more than 100 secret nuclear projects of the Iranian regime. Some of the more notable nuclear revelations include:

1. **June 1991:** Revealing the regime's preliminary nuclear facilities in Mo'alm Kalaye.

2. **October 1992:** Revealing the attempt to purchase nuclear warheads from Kazakhstan. The revelation aborted the shipment of the warheads to Iran.

3. **August 2002:** Revealing the uranium enrichment facility in Natanz, being the largest and most expansive of the regime's investment on its nuclear weapons program in a press conference in Washington, DC. The revelation disrupted Tehran's nuclear calculations and led IAEA inspections to Iran that confirmed the revelation;

4. **August 14, 2002:** Revealing the heavy water project in Arak in a press conference in Washington, DC.

5. **February 2003**: Revealing the most important companies involved in producing and importing equipment and necessary material for nuclear projects, including Kala Electric in Aab-Ali highway that was registered as a watch-making factory. However, this was actually

a center for centrifuge assembly and testing, and in an IAEA inspection, traces of highly enriched uranium were found at this site.

6. **May 2003:** Revealing the Lavizan-Shian Center. This was a very sensitive nuclear site for the regime and the mullahs immediately destroyed it and even removed the soil before allowing a June 2004 IAEA visit to the site.

7. **October 2003:** Revealing the Lashkarabad site and its front company (May 2003). This site was inspected by the IAEA, and the regime deceived the inspectors by taking them to another location.

8. **November 2003:** Revealing in November 2003, the special role of the IRGC in the nuclear projects clearly showed the military goals and aspects of this project.

9. **April 2004:** The NCRI revealed that Tehran had dedicated 400 nuclear experts to military industries.

10. **April 2004:** Exposing the new Center for Readiness and New Defense Technology (Lavizan-2). The equipment and activities from razed Lavizan site was moved to this site, but the site was kept off limits.

11. **September 2004:** NCRI revealed the allotment of $16bn to nuclear technology, purchase and smuggling of Deuterium from Russia, as well as details on the AEOI's companies;

12. **November 2004:** Revealing in a press conference in Paris the new technology center (Mojdeh site) and the names of their experts. In the conference, the Iranian resistance revealed the identity of Mohsen Fakhrizadeh, the key man of Iranian clandestine nuclear program who was kept secret until then. The IAEA has been insisting to interview Fakhrizaeh for the past few years, but the Iranian regime has not provided access.

13. **December 2004:** Revealing the Hemmat Missile Industries site in relation to produce nuclear chemical warheads.

14. **February 2005:** Revealing a project aimed at producing polonium-210 and beryllium to build nuclear bomb fuses.

15. **March 2005:** Revealing the secret nuclear center in the Parchin tunnel. This site focused on laser enrichment.

16. **May 2005:** Revealing the production and importing graphite necessary for nuclear bomb production.

17. **July 2005:** Revealing the import and production of Maraging steel to build the bomb fuselage and using it in centrifuge systems.

18. **August 2005:** Revealing the production of 4,000 ready-to-install centrifuges.

19. **August 2005:** Revealing in a press conference in Washington, DC, the meeting between Abdul Qadeer Khan, and commanders of the Iranian Revolutionary Guards in 1986 and 1987 in Tehran.

20. **August 2005:** Revealing in a press conference in Brussels the regime's plans to smuggle tritium from South Korea to increase nuclear explosion power.

21. **September 2005:** Revealing, in a Washington, DC, press conference, the regime's tunnel construction in its military centers to keep secret the material and equipment.

22. **September 2005:** Revealing in a press conference in Vienna that North Korean experts were helping the Iranian regime in developing warheads in Hemmat site in Khojir region, southeast of Tehran.

23. **November 2005**: In a press conference in Vienna, the NCRI revealed that the Iranian regime had taken the IAEA inspectors to another location than the one the UN nuclear watchdog was looking for at the sprawling Parchin military site.

24. **November 2005:** In a Washington, DC, press conference in, the NCRI revealed that Iran was building nuclear capable missiles in underground secret tunnels.

25. **December 2005:** In a press conference in Paris, the NCRI revealed the construction of a series of secret new sites, including one in Qom. Four years later it was established that site was Ferdow clandestine site, used for enriching uranium.

26. **January 2006:** Revealing importing of industrial press machines to shape enriched uranium in a bomb.

27. **August 2006:** Revealing the production of P2 centrifuges.

28. **September 2006:** Revealing in Washington, DC, the reactivation of laser enrichment projects.

29. **February 2007:** Revealing the specifications of 7 nuclear front companies related to the nuclear fuel cycle.

30. **September 2007:** Revealing a secret tunnel being constructed by the Ministry of Defense south of the Natanz site.

31. **February 2008:** Revealing the location of nuclear warhead construction in Khojeir and the nuclear weapon command center in Mojdeh.

32. **March 2008:** Revealing Beheshti University as a nuclear research center related to commanding weapons production in Mojdeh.

33. **September 2009:** Revealing Center of Explosion and Impact Technology (METFAZ) and changes in the nuclear command center.

34. **October 2009:** Revealing further details about the Fordow site.

35. **September 2010:** In Washington, D.C., the NCRI revealed a covert nuclear site located in tunnels in Behjatabad in the Abyek Township of Qazvin Province. This covert nuclear site was codenamed "311" and is known as Javadinia 2;

36. **April 2011:** The NCRI revealed in Washington, DC, the covert site near Tehran, named TABA, which was involved in production of centrifuge parts for tens of thousands of centrifuges. Tehran conceded the existence of this site the next day;

37. **July 2011:** Revealing in Washington, DC, the Defensive Innovation and Research Organization (SPND) nuclear bomb command center chaired by Mohsen Fakhrizadeh. SPND was later sanctioned by the Department of State in August 2014.

38. **January 2012**: Revealing 100 names of nuclear engineering experts active in various bomb making sections.

39. **April 2012:** Revealing in Washington, DC, further details of SPND operations, its involvement in the Fordow site, and the list of experts associated with this center.

40. **July 2013:** Revealing the top-secret Maadan Sharq nuclear site in Tehran's Damavand district.

41. **October 2013:** Revealing the relocation of Defensive Innovation and Research Organization (SPND) nuclear bomb command center.

42. **November 2013:** Revealing the "012" secret site in Isfahan's Mobarakeh linked to SPND.

43. **November 2014**: In a Washington, DC conference, revealing the Iranian regime's activities related to high explosive chambers at Parchin military site.

44. **February 2015:** Revealing in a press conference in Washington, DC, the existence of Lavizan-3 underground nuclear site in Tehran.

45. **May 2015:** NCRI Paris Office revealed the cooperation between the Iranian regime and North Korea regarding the nuclear weapons program of Iran and the presence of North Korean nuclear scientists in Tehran.

46. **June 2015:** Revealing Iran's deceitful tactics during nuclear negotiations with the P 5+1.

47. **September 2015:** Revealing Iran's cooperation with North Korea to deceive IAEA inspectors.

48. **December 2015:** Revealing how Iran laid out a plan to deceive the IAEA in its probe of Possible Military Dimensions of Iran's nuclear program.

49. **April 2017:** Revealing in press conference in Washington, DC, the status of the Iranian regime's nuclear bomb making apparatus, Plan-6 in the Parchin military complex operated by SPND.

50. **June 2017:** Revealing dozens of missile centers across Iran, including those who work in close collaboration with the nuclear bomb-making entity, SPND.

APPENDIX B

List of Publications by the National Council of Resistance of Iran, U.S. Representative Office

Terrorist Training Camps in Iran: How Islamic Revolutionary Guards Corps Trains Foreign Fighters to Export Terrorism

June 1017, 56 pages

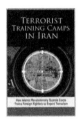

The book details how Islamic Revolutionary Guards Corps trains foreign fighters in 15 various camps in Iran to export terrorism. The IRGC has created a large directorate within its extraterritorial arm, the Quds Force, in order to expand its training of foreign mercenaries as part of the strategy to step up its meddling abroad in Syria, Iraq, Yemen, Bahrain, Afghanistan and elsewhere.

Presidential Elections in Iran:
Changing Faces; Status Quo Policies

May 2017, 78 pages

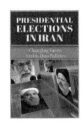

The book, reviews the past 11 presidential elections, demonstrating that the only criterion for qualifying as a candidate is practical and heartfelt allegiance to the Supreme Leader. An unelected vetting watchdog, the Guardian Council makes that determination.

The Rise of Iran's Revolutionary Guards' Financial Empire: How the Supreme Leader and the IRGC Rob the People to Fund International Terror

March 2017, 174 pages

This manuscript examines some vital factors and trends, including the overwhelming and accelerating influence (especially since 2005) of the Supreme Leader and the Islamic Revolutionary Guard Corps (IRGC). This study shows how ownership of property in various spheres of the economy is gradually shifted from the population writ large towards a minority ruling elite comprised of the Supreme Leader's office and the IRGC, using 14 powerhouses, and how the money ends up funding terrorism worldwide.

How Iran Fuels Syria War: Details of the IRGC Command HQ and Key Officers in Syria

November 2016, 74 pages

This book examines how the Iranian regime has effectively engaged in the military occupation of Syria by marshaling 70,000 forces, including the Islamic Revolutionary Guard Corps (IRGC) and mercenaries from other countries into Syria; is paying monthly salaries to over 250,000 militias and agents to prolong the conflict; divided the country into 5 zones of conflict and establishing 18 command, logistics and operations centers.

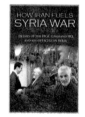

Nowruz 2016 with the Iranian Resistance: Hoping for a New Day, Freedom and Democracy in Iran

April 2016, 36 pages

This book describes Iranian New Year, Nowruz celebrations at the Washington office of Iran's parliament-in-exile, the National Council of Resistance of Iran. The yearly event marks the beginning of spring. It includes select speeches by dignitaries who have attended the NCRIUS Nowruz celebrations. This book also discusses the very rich culture and the traditions associated with Nowruz for centuries.

The 2016 Vote in Iran's Theocracy: An analysis of Parliamentary & Assembly of Experts Elections

February 2016, 70 pages

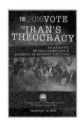

This book examines all the relevant data about the 2016 Assembly of Experts as well as Parliamentary elections ahead of the February 2016 elections. It looks at the history of elections since the revolution in 1979 and highlights the current intensified infighting among the various factions of the Iranian regime.

IRAN: A Writ of Deception and Cover-up: Iranian Regime's Secret Committee Hid Military Dimensions of its Nuclear Program

February 2016, 30 pages

The book provides details about a top-secret committee in charge of forging the answers to the International Atomic Energy Agency (IAEA) regarding the Possible Military Dimensions (PMD) of Tehran's nuclear program, including those related to the explosive detonators called EBW (Exploding Bridge Wire) detonator, which is an integral part of a program to develop an implosion type nuclear device.

Iranian Regime's Nuclear Duplicity: An Analysis of Tehran's Trickery in Talks with the P 5+1

January 2016, 74 pages

This book examines Iran's behavior throughout the negotiations process in an effort to inform the current dialogue on a
potential agreement. Drawing on both publicly available sources and those within Iran, the book focuses on two major periods
of intense negotiations with the regime: 2003-2004 and 2013-
2015. Based on this evidence, it then extracts the principles and
motivations behind Tehran's approach to negotiations as well
as the tactics used to trick its counterparts and reach its objectives.

Key to Countering Islamic Fundamentalism: Maryam Rajavi? Testimony To The U.S. House Foreign Affairs Committee

June 2015, 68 pages

Testimony before U.S. House Foreign Affairs Committee's
subcommittee on Terrorism, non-Proliferation, and Trade
discussing ISIS and Islamic fundamentalism. The book contains Maryam Rajavi's full testimony as well as the question
and answer by representatives.

Meet the National Council of Resistance of Iran

June 2014, 150 pages

Meet the National Council of Resistance of Iran discusses
what NCRI stands for, what its platform is, what it has done so
far, and why a vision for a free, democratic, secular, non-nuclear republic in Iran would serve the world peace.

How Iran Regime Cheated the World: Tehran's Systematic Efforts to Cover Up its Nuclear Weapons Program

June 2014, 50 pages

This book deals with one of the most fundamental challenges that goes to the heart of the dispute regarding the Iranian regime's controversial nuclear program: to ascertain with certainty that Tehran will not pursue a nuclear bomb. Such an assurance can only be obtained through specific steps taken by Tehran in response to the international community's concerns. The monograph discusses the Iranian regime's report  card as far as it relates to being transparent when addressing the international community's concerns about the true nature and the ultimate purpose of its nuclear program.

About NCRI-US

National Council of Resistance of Iran-US Representative Office acts as the Washington office for Iran's Parliament-in-exile, which is dedicated to the establishment of a democratic, secular, non-nuclear republic in Iran.

NCRI-US, registered as a non-profit tax-exempt organization, has been instrumental in exposing the nuclear weapons program of Iran, including the sites in Natanz, and Arak, the biological and chemical weapons program of Iran, as well as its ambitious ballistic missile program.

NCRI-US has also exposed the terrorist network of the Iranian regime, including its involvement in the bombing of Khobar Towers in Saudi Arabia, the Jewish Community Center in Argentina, its fueling of sectarian violence in Iraq and Syria, and its malign activities in other parts of the Middle East.

Our office has provided information on the human rights violations in Iran, extensive anti-government demonstrations, and the movement for democratic change in Iran.

Visit our website at **www.ncrius.org**

You may follow us on twitter @ncrius

Follow us on facebook NCRIUS

You can also find us on Instagram NCRIUS

CPSIA information can be obtained
at www.ICGtesting.com
Printed in the USA
BVOW10s0308201017
498038BV00015B/148/P